GET THE RING
KEEP THE RING

THE REALITY OF LOVE, SEX, & PURPOSE

ROOSEVELT WRIGHT, III

GET THE RING KEEP THE RING

ISBN-13: 978-0692336229

Printed in the United States of America.

Table of Contents

Foreword

Verified. Authentic, and TRUE are just a few of the choice words I use to describe Life Coach Roosevelt Wright and his commitment to Marriage. There is a blurred line of demarcation between reality and truth but Ro steps in with insight, wisdom, practical application, humor, fun, and good old fashioned advice to make the complex simple.

We live in a society where REAL people face REAL problems, REAL emotions, and REAL issues. Many are real tired of not understanding what's really happening in their lives. Many are even married yet they are still searching for real love. Some people find it – unfortunately though, the real way to love and fidelity has been choked out by all the real problems which threaten real relationships. The reality with Love and Marriage is that "real" has gone wrong.

Whether you are a young couple lacking the tangible example or a seasoned couple who needs to repair some of the wear and tear that life has stained on your relationship, "Get the Ring, Keep the Ring," will serve as an invaluable and practical tool.

Ro and his wife are an authentic couple whose transparency with love and life has helped to bring clarity, simplicity, truth, and success to everyone around them. In a world where people still place their hope in the joining of two hearts together it's important that we preserve marriage. As you read the pages of this book, allow the energy and spirit of unboxed wisdom to infuse you with insight, laughter, and hope. This book will be a treasure for many generations to come.

Nikki Brooks, International Motivational Speaker & Author

1
Magic

Every man is capable of cheating. From the Pastor you assume is so Spiritual, to the Father who has been your idea man all your life, no man is exempt. Every woman is capable of being promiscuous. Even your mother who appears to be so innocent and humble. She too has a breaking point. All it takes is a weak hour in a Season of Testing. We are all capable of taking a chance in the wrong direction. The key is to reduce those chances for the person you love.

We are human, and because of this fact it is our nature to be seduced in the flesh. Even the most Religious must agree, curiosity has existed since the beginning of time. It was the influence of a naked woman that enticed a man enough to break the promise he had previously made with his Creator. Don't be mad at him. He was hungry and blinded by her curves. He couldn't help himself.

Sex is interesting. It's why men watch porn videos. Most men who watch porn videos have no intention of cheating on their wives. The curiosity of sex is just in him. It's been in him and it's never going away. While men attempt to hide their sexual curiosities from their significant others men would be surprised to know women are just as curious about sex as men are.

The penis comes in many different sizes, shapes, colors, and forms. Girls grow up rarely seeing a real live actual lovestick. The first time she sees one in the flesh she has instantly opened the door for curiosity. She will want to either see that one again or see a different one. The more of them she sees the more interesting they become to her. This is why women have a preferred size. Curiosity makes them wonder if the shape and size of a man's penis will make the love experience more interesting.

Breasts and Vaginas are different on every woman. Young boys grow up hearing about them and they anticipate the opportunity to see them for real. When he gets that opportunity, he will either want to see hers again or see other ones. The more of them he sees, the more curious he becomes. It's why men have a preferred breast size and a picture of an idea butt in their heads. He wonders what another one will feel like, look like, and even move like.

When he gets the opportunity to place his *tool* in a *toolbox* the feeling is addictive. He wants to feel it again and he also wants to know if it feels the same way with all women. The more sex he has he learns every woman's body is different while developing a taste for the kind of women he likes. It's a Symptom of the Flesh.

You Should Want It All The Time

It is interesting and its exciting. So, stop acting like there are better things to do with your time. There isn't. If people could do so and not feel inappropriate most people would walk around naked all day just to feel the wind seduce the skin and blow against the inner thigh. The smell of masculinity turns a woman on. The aroma of a woman's sweetness entices a man. Even though clothes are required in public, don't you for a second think a woman doesn't see a fine hunk of a man and wonder what he looks like naked. Men can see an attractive woman covered from her head to her toes and he will still imagine what she must look like naked. Don't be mad at him. He can't help it and neither can she.

A man's interest in sexual pleasure has nothing to do with his heart or his Integrity. Sexuality can be a Weapon of Mass

8

Destruction. All a man has to do is smell the opportunity to taste it and he will be distracted. This is why there are dress codes in the workplace. It's why seductively suggestive outfits are frowned upon in sacred settings. Decisions can be persuaded even in the courtroom by seductive appearances. It's why the educational system embraces the idea of school uniforms in most states. The interest is embedded in our flesh and all we can do is reduce the chances we have to give into it.

Symptoms Of The Flesh

Why wouldn't a man want to see a woman's breasts? He knows Nations and Democracies have been built and torn down by the power of the breast. These two utensils are used to nurture babies and every man has a need for sexual nurturing. The woman's breasts contain a hidden power that can make a preacher lose track of the Holy Ghost and a Politician make the most immoral decisions while he's in office. Truth be told, the real power is in the imagination. Because she knows it, she has learned she doesn't even have to exhibit all of her breast to retain a man's attention. She just simply has to wear a blouse exposing merely the surface of her cleavage. She knows he'll imagine what the rest of her breasts must look like. And she knows she doesn't have to say a word or even look at him. All she has to do is push them up and walk slowly past him. His eyes will wander and she will control his mind if for no more than the three seconds it took for her to walk pass him. It's a Symptom Of The Flesh.

Why wouldn't a woman want to see a man's joystick? She knows seeds of life are manufactured within it. It gives her an idea of his strength. His power. His magic. He has an extension cord that is waiting to be plugged into a wall and she'd like to provide him a power outlet. To tell you the truth, the power is in her imagination. He knows if his physique is right he can talk to her through a Stafford shirt without even using his vocal cords. He knows the right walk and the right smell can cause her to peek at him out of the corner of her eye even if she is in the middle of a conversation with someone else. In that moment. Just that quick. She has already given him enough to know if he wants it and is willing to put in the work, he can get it. A woman likes magic. Magic is filled with surprises. No matter how conservative she is, all women like to see what kind of rabbit he will pull out of his hat. It's a Symptom of her Flesh.

She's not a whore. She's not a freak. She is just a woman who has given more power to her Flesh than The Spirit.

In The Flesh, we believe Sex is the complete definition of a person. It's why we assume sex is the remedy for loneliness and the description of friendship. Sex may attract you to someone but it won't keep you with them. Most women will tell you, great sex from a lazy man eventually plays out. Great sex from a woman with a nasty attitude will eventually drive a man away.

Curiosity

We are fleshy by nature. We're human. We were made from dirt. That's why we are easily attracted to that 'dirty stuff'. Women are curious to know what his touchdown will feel like in her end zone. Some players break the line and rush up the middle. Some players are tight ends. Some players are wide open, while others... you have to watch them. When you least expect they'll catch her off guard with a Quarterback Sneak. Ultimately, she is just curious to find out if he will slowly work his way up her field or if he is a quick three and out. She's curious to know if his body can back up what his appearance was saying to her and he can get it again if he makes the conversion after he scores the touchdown.

He wants to look in her eyes to see what makes her lips tremble and her eyes roll like a pool table's high balls. He studies her waves because he knows rivers move in a pattern when the current gets stronger. He watches her eyes because he knows it doesn't matter if she is lying on the floor or a bed, the pupil doesn't lie when it is surprised by something majestic. He will enter the

10

cave of her thighs so perfectly just to see if she can contain the power he is giving her body while knowing only the soul can respond to such a force. The sound of her breathing becomes the motivation for energy stored up to be released like waves of electricity. He shocks her intimately knowing he has lit up every corner of darkness in her body and he is grateful she allowed him to store his baseball bat in her dugout.

It's sex. It's magic. It's a human necessity. When two people meet, conversation cuts out the picture but sex ultimately nails the picture to the wall. Most people think about sex a million times more than they actually have it. So you have to ask yourself, are you upset that others are having it a lot or are you upset because you aren't getting it enough? Ice cream melts without a freezer and relationships freeze if they don't stay heated. Talk as much as you can but a relationship without sexual fantasy is a space heater that doesn't heat the room. At some point, you will either fix the heater or somebody will want to switch rooms.

That Good Sex

The key for us is to remember the Purpose of Sex. Most importantly, it is the Path for Reproduction. Anything used in an incorrect manner will eventually backfire. A man can either sit at the Head of His Table or he can sit in a chair on Maury. We are sleeping with each other so rapidly the economy can't keep up with the demand. The population is growing faster than our abilities to provide for the products of good sex. Many of us are so selfish that we want that "Good Sex" even if it's irresponsible sex.

Secondly, Sex is the ability to build Chemistry. It illuminates love and affection for two people who are committed to each other. We're like tech devices. It's in our settings mode to find chemistry in each other. It's supposed to be a by-product of Commitment but hackers always find a way to navigate around the factory settings.

When a woman gives her body to a man without Commitment it means she honors a moment more than she honors the rest of her life. When a man seeks a woman who will allow him to sleep with her without a Commitment he is no different than an animal. Interesting though, animals have more respect for their female counterparts than men have for women.

Lastly, it's Ministry. Two people touch, agree, and empower each other. Ministry is simply the ability to meet the Internal Needs of someone else. A man meets the internal needs of his wife. A wife meets the internal needs of her husband. It's magical how a woman can sleep with different men but only one completely fulfills her internal needs. Ask any women. She can separate the two. She knows when she has been *sexed and* she knows when her body has been taken on a magical escapade. She is only satisfied with the ghetto because no man has ever taken her to Paris.

The kiss feels different when the heart is behind it. A touch feels different when affection is in it. Sounds come out differently when the chemistry is magical. Afterall, when a man waves his wand and lays his abrakadabra on you, you're supposed to be surprised. The worst magician is the one who does a trick you've already seen someone else do.

The truth about magic is that it's not really a trick. Magicians simply attract your attention to one thing while preparing another thing you aren't expecting. Good Sex is the activity which satisfies the desires of the flesh while simultaneously meeting the needs of the heart.

2
Preseason

Most women have read too many Fairy Tales. By 7th Grade they are already imagining what their dream life will be. By 12, a young girl has already decided what she associates with "cute". She can tell you who is cute in her class and who is ugly. Most mothers would be surprised to know their 12 year old already have an idea of who is sexy. If she knows what sexy looks like at 12 then before she gets out of high school she will be tempted to find out how sexy feels.

Cinderella

Young girls really do believe the person they fall in love with in Middle School is the person they are going to marry. It happens for less than 1% of the people in the world. Hardly anybody marries their middle school crush. Girls see themselves in their Cinderella dresses and the cute boy who sits three desks in front of her in second period class is the Prince Charming in her mind. That's why she can't stay focused in class. She is daydreaming about her dream wedding. She is doodling hearts and love pictures all over her notebooks while thinking about him.

Boys are no different. I used to wait on the JET Magazine to come in the mail every week just to sneak a peek at the Beauty of the Week. Me and my friends didn't care about anything in the magazine other than that one page. Even though the lady wore a swimsuit on the picture in the magazine it was still transparent to our eyes. Our imaginations saw right through it. By Middle School we had already advanced to porn magazines we stole from older cousins.

A Porn Magazine to a young boy is like the Holy Bible to Grandma. It was our daily inspiration. Don't clean your 14 year old son's room. Tell him to do it. If you go cleaning under his bed you'll find all kind of sticky socks and magazines with a few of the pages stuck together from a different kind of glue. By high school young boys are already trying to make the ideas he saw in the smut magazine come to life.

While the little girls were hoping to be Cinderella, happily in love with her Prince Charming, all the boys only wanted one thing. We just wanted to see Cinderella naked.

Driving

Women always control the date. It doesn't matter who asked who out. It doesn't matter who picked the restaurant or who is paying for the meal. Nothing will happen on a date that the woman doesn't allow to happen. A man can say all the right words. He can be smoother than peanut butter on bread but if she has already decided in her mind she is not having sex then most likely he's not getting any jelly to go with that peanut butter tonight.

However, if she shows any sign of weakness it is the nature of a man to explore it. When a woman is dating she is under construction. A few potholes from her past are being restored. She shouldn't have sex with a man if God is still fixing the road.

Don't say things on a date which will make him speculate how he can possibly ranger his way through parts of the woods which make you feel uncomfortable. It's uncomfortable to you for a reason. Talking about certain things authorize unwanted emotions to answer when the *teacher calls the roll*. You like what he is saying and you don't want him to know you like it but your facial expressions, voice tone, and body language has already told him to keep pushing that button.

Most men will drive in the middle of the street if it weren't for the lane dividers. Men will try to be a Gentleman but if it looks like he can be a Freak too he'll drive in the middle of the street until he sees which lane is the easiest to stay in. It's the woman's job to control traffic on a date. He's going to drive all over the place until he sees that sign telling him All Traffic Must Merge Into One Lane. Put him in the lane you want him to stay in until Construction is complete on the other side.

Elevators

You must remember. The man you date may be an adult but all men still have a remnant of that young smut magazine boy in him. He may be mature and well groomed, polite and kind with the attributes of a gentlemen. Don't you let maturity and first impressions fool you. With the exception of very few men, if he thinks he can get you in bed on the first night he is going to do everything in his power to push the right button. He may have even began the night with the best intentions but if you take him down Possibility Blvd. all etiquette essentials are thrown out of the window. He has no problem driving down that street.

It's like getting on an elevator. I walk in and right before the door closes a sexy woman walks in. She and I are the only two people on the elevator. We have small talk and generic conversation about the weather. I feel a vibe from her that she is digging me. We make eye contact in THAT way. You know "that" way. Now, I know I'm going to the 17th floor but I wait to see what number she presses on the Button Panel. If she presses 19, guess what, all of sudden... I'm pressing 19 too.

If a woman even makes a man think he can get it he will change his plans immediately. The floor she is on might be a little more exciting than the floor he was going to. Even if he follows her to her floor, everything that happens on that floor is what she allows to happen. However, women must be careful. You can't lead a man to your kitchen. Tell him he can have some of your cereal. Let him pour cereal and milk in a bowl then just as he lifts the spoon to his mouth you tell him he can't have any of it until later. No way Hosea. If you didn't want him to have your cereal you shouldn't have even allowed him to open the box.

Laying The Groundwork

When a man is really interested in a woman and he wants it to work with her he will not allow her to manipulate him on the first date no matter how tempted he is to have sex with her. Don't let these church girl goodie two shoes fool you. At times many of them can be the most trifling products on the market. They pretend to be innocent but they already know before dating somebody if they are willing to sleep with him on the first night or not. Surprisingly, today's women are more likely to initiate sex faster than men are.

If a man wants a real relationship with you he is not going to have sex with you even if he knows he can. For men, it's about establishing leadership. If he wants it to work then he is also going to want it to work on his terms.

If you want to see a man with swagger look for the man who knows a woman wants him in the most sexual way but he has rearranged the control factor to work to his advantage. She can't have him until he wants her to have him. It drives her crazy because she is used to having it her way. Now, she can't understand why the very things which have worked for all her other love interests is not working for this one. He has her right where he wants her. His mystery will just attract her to him even more.

He knows the minute he gives her what she wants the relationship will change. She knows the minute she gets what she wants the relationship may become the exact replica of all her previous relationships. Holding out and exercising discipline will strangely force her interest toward his mind rather than his sex. He has her right where he wants her. It will be the beginning of a beautiful future where he has trained her from day one that she can't manipulate him. From that day forward she begins to trust that he is capable of making her stronger in her most desperate areas of weakness.

Sex controls most relationships because it's what they were built on. If your relationship has been structured by Discipline since Day One then there is a great possibility that discipline will continue to strengthen you through the years. It doesn't make sense to lick all the icing up before the cake is ready. It was designed to go on the cake. Let the cake finish baking. You'll eventually get the cake and the icing as well.

3
The Experience

In your adolescent years, you hadn't had much experience with the opposite sex. So, the person you admired had the strangest effects on you. If the person walked past you on a school hallway it made you blush. Just touching that person's hand could send electricity through your body. You'd find yourself daydreaming during class just thinking about that person's smile.

Water Park

Your first kiss was special. Monumental even.

Your lips actually touched another person's lips! The only thing your lips were used to touching was food. Now, you have touched somebody's lips and magically slid your tongue in their mouth as they slid theirs in your mouth. There were blasts of energy spreading to all the wrong places on your bodies at the same time. You are never ever in your life going to forget that moment.

Before you knew it you were sweating. Yes, you were dripping in perspiration. If you ever go to a water park you'll see these gigantic water slides. You climb the stairs to the top of the slide. It looks like a long way down but as soon as you sit down it only takes a few seconds to get to the bottom. Well, that's exactly how fast the sweat from your chest area slid down to your stomach as you kissed.

For some reason, your finger tips were damp. The palms of your hands were soggy dishrags. You looked around and there weren't even any doors or windows opened but you felt a draft behind your ear. It cooled the back of your neck as sweat dripped from your hair. Breasts rubbing against his chest were as clothes hanging in a packed closet... not even breathing room. Both person's eyes dangled into a neverland of space. The anticipation had built up so intensely that while standing there necking for 45 minutes with your clothes on you reached a climax just from the velocity of desire.

That's when kissing felt like Heaven and a touch from the person you loved could save you from all fears. If you pay close attention to that First Kiss Experience the kiss did not create the magic. The magic was created from ignorance. You had no idea what would happen next but two people decided to take the adventure together.

Don't Let It Get Boring

Adventure isn't supposed to stop once you're married.

The reason your first kiss feels so electric is because you had never experienced it before. It is important that married couples try new things. Life gets boring very quick. Careers and daily responsibilities will capture you and keep you so tied up until life becomes a routine rather than an experience.

Everything in life should be an Experience.

Parenting should be an experience. It gets so hard at times that we treat it as a chore but it should be an experience. Every day you get to find new ways to make your child smile. You get to explore new options to shape your child's mind. You get to cook for your child to see what foods energize him and which foods don't sit well with his body. You get to see what kind of girls he's attracted to and watch him develop into a young man. You are given the opportunity to watch your daughter mature and hopefully have more opportunities in life than you have.

Your Career should be an experience. You should always be motivated to work. That's why it's important to have a career that will truly interest you. As human beings we improve daily. Each day we stretch our minds further and further. Our capabilities expand. Companies grow because over time they experience new ways to produce and more inexpensive ways to do it. It's a day by day process which profits you great insight and perspective as you mature within your career.

Your Spirituality is an experience. When we're weighed down our Faith is built. We become stronger through our struggles. Some people meditate to keep themselves spiritually strong and it works for them. Many pray and prayer works for them. There is an indescribable feeling when you pray about something and feel it removed from your Spirit. You learn your Faith as you put it to work. As you defeat obstacles you become one with your Faith and it surprises you how much stronger you have become over time. The things which usually defeat you are now easily defeated by you.

Sex should be an experience. The absolute worst thing a couple can do is have routine sex. Spice it up! It's supposed to electrify you. The way the feeling of your first kiss abducted you is the same way sex should feel EVERY SINGLE TIME. Watch videos, read books... do whatever you have to do keep your bedroom interesting.

Your spouse should anticipate sex with you all day. There should be a wonder in your mind of what you'll try next. Look for new areas on each other's body to explore. Seek new positions to demonstrate on each other. If the place you make love looks the same after you're done then you haven't done anything.

Ignorant Expectation is beneficial to your sexual maturity. You aren't supposed to know what to expect but you are supposed to expect something fulfilling. Take turns. One night it should be the husband's responsibility to innovate the lovespace. The next time it should be the wife's obligation to introduce something new. Keep it going. If your mind is on new ways to seduce each other then you don't have time to seduce anyone else. Sex with you should be such an anticipated experience that your spouse wonders what on Earth you will come up with next.

When your relationship is reduced to an obligated affair your attention will easily be distracted. While marriage is full of responsibilities it should never feel like an obligation. Responsibilities are the works I volunteer to complete for the benefit of my marriage. Obligations are things I really don't want to do or even agree with but I'll do it just to keep peace. It's like working a job you hate but you do it because it pays rent. There's no life in that. Life should be full of experiences which make us excited to wake up and breathe again the next day.

4

Preferences

Most of us have seen too many movies. Not too many women in this lifetime will get to be Julia Roberts and attract a millionaire who will sweep her off the streets and shower her with expensive gifts. If you're 40 and still waiting on it to happen you need to wake up. Pinch yourself. It was just a movie.

The world is filled with single women and men who have done everything "right", but are somehow still single. A person can pass enough tests to get a college degree, a great paying job, a nice home, and a great vehicle, but can't seem to pass anyone's compatibility test. It is hurtful and even depressing at times. Then, just as you do something to take your mind off your loneliness another one of your friends calls you screaming because they are now engaged. It makes you want to stay in bed all day and never leave your house.

People always tell you you're attractive. They always tell you how successful you are. They always come to you for advice. It makes you wonder, "If I'm so special then why can't I find anybody?" You're not alone. Millions of women and men are on the same boat as you... successful people with success in every area of their life except Love.

Social Sites

Social Media has become phenomenal in many ways. They are great for staying connected with friends. It's easier to send a letter to someone on Facebook than it is to mail an actual letter. You can see pictures of distant family and friends instantly. These

23

are a few of the things we have grown to love about the Social Sites. However, we forget the main reason Social Networks even began.

Facebook started on a college campus. Mark Zuckerberg only wanted to find a way for college students on the Harvard campus to meet each other. Single people needed to know who else was single. What's better than a website for single people to meet other single people?

As the site grew, even married people joined the fun. They found the site an easy way to fellowship with their friends as well. When the site became just as popular to married people as it was to single people they developed a way for you to identify which group you belonged to on the site. A status option gives you the opportunity to select Married, Single, or In A Relationship. It's important because people who may like you can either get a green light, yellow light, or the red light.

Proceed

People don't know you're available unless you make it known. When you drive, the green light tells you it's okay to continue proceeding. When you go to a store there is usually a sign somewhere that says "Open". Even when I take my kids Trick Or Treating I tell them if a person has a light on it's a sign to enter their yard. Homes without a light are also giving a sign. Do not enter.

When you're dating, you must give a sign that you are open for business. People can tell when a sign is encouraging them to proceed. They also know when there is no sign, chances are you're not open. They will drive past you.

Be willing to mingle in different circles. If you stay around the same people all the time you won't meet many new people. You may have to go to places you rarely go. That restaurant you always said you wanted to dine in is a start. Consider hearing a local band play. Usually the band members have large support groups. Many of them are single. Community events and programs usually have different types of people. Many are single. Surprisingly, the library is a great place to bump into someone. Usually at libraries, people read alone.

Even if you like going to clubs don't go to the same clubs repeatedly. Bounce around a little bit. Fresh ground produces fresh fruit.

Church is also a great place to meet interesting people especially if it's a church fellowship. Consider visiting a church function with a friend. You never know who you will stumble upon. If you are a parent become more active in your child's school. You'd be surprised how many Single Parents are involved in their children's school. Most of the schools have Parent Groups. In one conversation you'll know instantly who is single and who is married. Something interesting could be brewing but waiting on you to stir the pot.

Checklists

Never attempt to date with a Preference Chart embedded in your head. We all have an idea of the kind of person we'd like to meet but don't limit your happiness to a list. Your checklist isn't created by experience. It's formed out of expectation. Expectations are formed out of desire. You have a fantasy and you form a criteria in your mind from those ideals.

When you do this you automatically scan every room you enter for the picture you have in your mind. If you don't see that person you turn everyone else off. Don't do that. The perfect person may not meet every variable on your checklist of preferences. You are single because your fantasy hasn't become a reality. You could be in a relationship if you would allow reality to become a fantasy.

You may desire your idea person to be tall. What if the right person for you has everything you're looking for but just happens to be short? Don't ignore all their other potentials just because one thing on your list was unmet. "Perfect" doesn't mean everything is correct. Hear the word as a verb rather than an adjective. Never look for a perfect person. Look for the person who can perfect you.

Be willing to work around a few of the desires on your list because it is almost impossible you will find someone who meets every expectation of your fantasy checklist. When you get to know someone's heart your list of variables will magically change. It's why people of the opposite race have success. It's why people from different financial upbringings have been able to make it work. It's why people with opposite educational accomplishments find ways to make it last. When you truly find love the exterior things are upstaged by the interior potentials you don't see when you first meet someone.

Batteries

Our eyes and our hearts should be led by our Purpose. There is something you were created to do in this realm of existence. It's your Spiritual Definition. The only person you should even consider settling with is the person who fits into that definition. Many times that person won't look like the image you have convinced yourself is your dream person. Many times they may be missing some key pieces to their own life. You will know it immediately because the parts they are missing will be the parts you possess already.

Purpose is that Christmas gift you get which needs a battery to operate. You have the gift but it's not going to work without a battery. Sometimes, people give you the battery with the gift but it's the wrong battery. The person you settle with is your battery. Make sure they fit your purpose.

Spend less time looking for a cute person. Spend more time looking for an acute person. That cute person will have you running in circles like a cat with a ribbon tied to it's tail. An acute person will be sharp and sensitive enough to meet your needs.

Spend less time looking for a wealthy person. Spend more time looking for a rich person. Someone with a lot of money may be able to fill your closet but could be clueless when it comes to fulfilling your heart. The person who can enrich you will last longer than the person who is rich in materialism.

Innergy

There is a reason the Christmas gift won't work without the battery. The battery is it's source of energy. Everything around us operates by energy. The person for you is the person who can inner-gize you. Love should make you better. You can narrow your options down a whole lot by simply asking yourself, "Out of all the people I date, who makes me feel better about myself?"

Some people know how to have a good time. You feel good when you're with them. However, the most valuable person is the person who leaves a remnant when they aren't even around you. This person doesn't just make you feel better. They make you feel better about yourself. There is a difference.

Don't look for obvious popular desires. Everybody wants someone attractive. Everybody dating is looking for someone with money. These are average preferences. They are also the reason so many people are still single. Physical attributes change very quickly. People gain weight, have life changing accidents, depreciate in health, have kids, and get hurt on the job everyday.

Physical Appearance better not be higher on your checklist than Character and Humility.

Go in any nightclub. There are a lot of pretty, single people. They look good on the outside but many are pretty messy on the inside. Nine times out of ten if you were honest with yourself you are one of those people or have been in your past. Learn to give others the same chance you feel you deserve. The very mistakes you attempt to cover up are the same faults they are covering up as well. No matter how attractive someone else is to you, your soul has a criteria that your eyes sometimes fail to comprehend.

5
Smiles

Don't ever allow people to determine what makes you happy. There is more than one recipe for Happiness.

For some people, Sex is the priority ingredient for Happiness. There is absolutely nothing wrong with it at all. It just makes you wonder how many people they'd have to sleep with to determine which sexual partner makes them the happiest. But, at least they made their choice without it being manipulated by someone else's definition of Happiness.

Truth is, life changes over time. It may only take a box of chocolates to make you happy after a long work day. However, the death of a loved one may require much more to generate a smile. The longer you live the more you will appreciate the little things which employ smiles. Valuable people are the people who know exactly what to do to make you happy beyond sex.

It's why you fall for someone in the first place. The person who has mastered how to keep you smiling most of the day will always win your heart over the person who only makes you smile during sex.

The smile is an outward display representing the satisfaction of the spirit. It says your Soul agrees. The person who knows how to keep you smiling will more than likely take care of your heart. It's pathetic how we make Sex a higher priority than Love. You can't have sex all day. Love is something you can't hide. It's with you everywhere you go.

The Difference Between Sex and Love

Sex is something you can improve by experience. Love lifts the perimeters off of sex. You can have sex with anybody. Love just simply makes the sexual experience even more significant.

There are people who feel Love is overrated. It is their opinion Sex and Love are equal necessities. However, on your dying bed you would most likely rather see the person you confidently love rather than random people you've sporadically had sex with throughout your life.

Love and Sex are never equal. Sex may make you feel good for the moment but love has potential to last forever. Smiles are good to have but if truth be told what we're all really looking for is Joy. You may enjoy a sexual encounter but Love opens the door to a joy with the possibility of lasting forever.

You Can Learn A Lot From Old People...

Whenever I see an old couple I smile. They have a magnetic effect on my heart. I am completely humbled by a marriage in it's 60th Anniversary. It's hard to just stay in good health for 60 years nevertheless be married for 60 years. The Golden Years are full of smiles. When you have survived so much together you learn to just smile through it all.

The older couple's smile is an outward expression of inner completion. Their smile says "we beat it all." They have endured every test and defeated every challenge. They were not concerned with profiting money. Their greatest reward is their smile. They don't have to worry about the little things which defeat many younger marriages. They've survived them. They don't have to worry if the other spouse is tempted to cheat. They are too old to even care if they do.

Death, Health Attacks, Financial Holes, Infidelity, and Sexual Frustration will all persistently hunt you throughout your life. In the end, being able to survive it all together implants a smile in your heart that your face can't help but illuminate at all times.

Smile Ms. Celie

In Steven Spielberg's movie The Color Purple, Whoopi Goldberg portrays Ms. Celie. The housewife of "Mister". She was taunted, called ugly and made to believe nobody liked her. Negativity had been implanted in her mind for so long she had nothing to smile about.

She and her husband's mistress shared a much needed conversation in Celie's bedroom about self esteem. Shug Avery, the mistress, stood Celie in front of a mirror and dared her to smile. Celie covered her mouth. Shug Avery pulled her hands away from her face and told her she had a pretty smile. Immediately, Celie showed her teeth and gave the biggest smile in years.

Afterwards, Celie confides in Shug Avery. She tells Ms. Avery even though her husband climbs on top of her every night to have sex with her it felt as if someone was going to the bathroom on her. Shug tells her, if that's what she feels making love is then she is still a virgin.

The Best Cookies

Sex doesn't guarantee you a smile and it doesn't always mean you are loved. Just because people have sex doesn't mean the complete need of the person is being fulfilled. Maybe the sexual need is fulfilled but the needs of the heart are still incomplete. Sex doesn't even feel like Love. Sex just feels like... Sex. I didn't say it doesn't feel good. It just doesn't feel like Love.

I love Great American Cookies. Sometimes I stop by the cookie counter in the mall and order a few cookies. I usually get the Peanut Butter cookies which are already shelved. They are good. However, one time I stopped by the cookie counter and they were putting fresh cookies on the shelf tender and hot, just out of the oven. Even though both cookies were round and brown there was a difference.

Sex is the cookie that's always on the shelf. You can get that whenever you want it. It's always available. But, you have to be in the right place at the right time for the cookie that's hot. You eat the cookie from the shelf and forget all about it when you're done. The hot cookie makes you close your eyes and smile. THAT, my friend, is Love.

6
Pictures

Your family's opinion of the person you're dating is shaped by what you tell them long before they meet the person you're dating.

These people know you. You can't fool them. They will know instantly if you're making a mistake. They will also know if the person you are dating is good for you. They have decades of experience dealing with you, living with you, and understanding how you work. In their minds, they know you better than you know yourself.

Roomates

Your very first roommates are your family members. They already know you don't pick up behind yourself so there's no sense in convincing them you and an OCD person are going to work out. If you are from a Christian family and you have fallen in love with a person who has a completely different perception of God, no matter how much you fool yourself your family will see the irregularity in your relationship in the midst of your blindness.

You can't force your mother to accept a person she feels is a bad rhythm for you. A father will have a hard time accepting a man whom he feels will be the downfall of his daughter's life. Your parents and siblings can sum up their opinion of the person you are dating after one conversation. They are overprotective because they care.

The people you grew up with have seen you cry. They are also the very people who helped you recover. They are the people who watched you find yourself. They are also the people who saw you stumble but forgave you. They have devoted a lot of time assisting your maturity. They have played a valuable role in you becoming the perfect picture you think you are today.

Cigarettes and Mean Eyes

My wife was raised in a Single Parent Home. Her mother is the rock of their family. When I proposed to my wife, in excitement she said "Yes!" I thought the hard part was over. Minutes later she told me it wouldn't be official until after I met her mother. That didn't even bother me. I've always been favored by mothers. I figured it would be a piece of cake.

I didn't realize she was raised by her mother and all her aunts. So, when she suggested I would have to get her mother's approval she meant I had to get the approval of her mother AND her aunts. I will never forget the first time I met them all.

I was asked to sit down at the dining room table in the home of the matriarch of their family. In came all these women with ash trays. It was very quiet. I could tell by their eyes my boat wasn't about to smooth sail on these waters. My Mother In Law pulled out a lighter and a cigarette. As she lit the cigarette she looked directly into my eyes. The room was more silenced than a library. Looking dead in my face, she exhaled smoke and very calmly asked, "Who yo people son?"

My wife attempted to answer for me and her mother sternly interrupted her, "I didn't ask you. I asked him." My wife politely closed her mouth and her aunt gently prompted her to take a seat. I began to answer and her aunt interjected, "Oh I know yo daddy. He's a good man. He does a lot with the youth in community."

34

Right when I assumed I was home-free her mother blew out another puff and said, "That don't mean nothing to me."

It was quiet all over again.

By now, I think all the sisters were smoking. It was like a competition or something. I tried to clear my throat and her aunt asked, "What? Do you have a problem with me smoking in my house?" Very quickly I responded, "Oh no ma'am. Not at all."

Her mother asked, "So what are your intentions for my baby? She is in Nursing School and what makes you think I'm gonna allow you to distract her off of the path that we have been working hard to accomplish?"

As I explained to her my future plans included her daughter her mother slowly came around. By the end of the evening we were laughing and looking at baby pictures of my wife. It didn't matter how old my wife was. Her mother still saw her as the precious, little, bony girl on her baby pictures. She was not about to let any man distort those images which were still in her mind.

Before we left, my Mother In Law told me, "I'm pretty good at judging people's character. I guess you're alright. We'll see. Just know I got my eye on you." I grinned and responded, "Yes Ma'am."

All Eyes Are On You

Family may accept your decision but that doesn't mean they aren't ready to go to war with your fiance at any moment. This is why it's important you never share temporary details about your relationship with your family. Every relationship will have struggles. You'll have to purge through together. Some events in your marriage will only be healed by time. There is no sense in telling others about it... especially your family.

In the beginning, your family is only concerned with you. They haven't known the person you're dating as long as you have. They also don't know specific details about that person which you have been privileged to learn. They only know what you expose to them. If you call a family member and tell them about a fight you've had it is human nature to tell the story from your point of view. Unless you have a track record of lying your family will most likely share your view because they know you better than the person you are dating.

The downfall of sharing your business with your family early in your relationship is your family's first impression of the person you love is the picture you paint for them. If every time you talk to your mother you share something negative your mother will begin to think negatively about the person you're dating. If you share something positive then your family will think positive about the person. It's good to be balanced. If you're going to tell them the bad things you're going through then also tell them the good things. A balanced opinion helps to prohibit attacks when you really need an unbiased opinion in future situations.

Insist Inclusion

In-Laws will only include your spouse equally when you insist they do. You must almost literally enforce inclusion upon them by excluding yourself from family ventures if your spouse is not welcomed. They will eventually learn they can't have you without also having your spouse. One thing is for certain. If they really love you they will deal with whomever you love rather than risk losing you altogether. They may not like the ultimatum you have given them but they will just have to accept your terms. It's only fair.

We don't get to love each other only when we make good decisions. Love is sticking by your family member even when they can't see what lies ahead. If the walls fall down on them, true love is being right there to help them pick up every fallen brick. Sometimes, we all learn the hard way but being blindly in love with someone shouldn't mean I go through a learning process without my family's love. If I've made a bad choice then eventually I will realize it.

What makes a family picture special are the stories every member can tell about each other but they loved each other through it all.

Competition

Probably the worst thing a woman can do to her husband is run to her father for everything she needs. Similarly, the worst thing a man can do is run to his mother for everything.

Your man is auditioning to be your first and last source for everything you need. Real men take pride in being able to provide for and cover his woman. It actually makes him more responsible when he knows there is someone trusting and depending on him at all times. However, no man wants to compete with his woman's father. It's a battle he can't win. It makes him feel small.

If a woman tells her father everything going on in her life, asks him for money, and asks him for advice before she considers her husband's opinion then maybe she should move back in with daddy and marry him. There are only two reasons a woman should value her father's perspective over her husband. Either her man is heavily under the influence of substance abuse and he doesn't make rational sense anymore or if he has developed a pattern of lying and she can't tell when he is truthful at all anymore.

A woman wants to be her man's source of strength and compassion. She is not trying to compete with his mother. One of the easiest ways to push your woman away is to tell your mother everything going on in your relationship.

Girls have it hard enough trying to break away from their own mother's handcuffs just to be with the man they love. They are not trying to break away from one chain to be controlled again by a Mother In Law. A man can pay every bill in the house but it's one thing he must understand. Your home is always HER house. A woman never wants other people to know what's going on in HER house... especially not her man's mother.

The minute a man tells his mother how late his wife comes in the house his mother's mind will begin to wander in a neck of the woods she may not even need to be scouting in. The day a woman tells her father they are short on the rent because her husband has been irresponsible with the money she has officially given him permission to watch every dime she and her husband spend.

A woman prefers her man to talk to her rather than his mother. His Mother In Law already feels she knows her son better than his woman does and his woman doesn't want to feel defeated whenever she has to understand how her man works. You're supposed to be learning each other together.

A relationship is strengthened when a man gets the support of his wife's parents and his wife gets support from his parents.

As One

When you marry someone you become one. It means your family is your spouse's family. Your business is now your spouse's business. Your spouse's family is now your family as well. When you establish to your family that you are one they will respect you as one.

If your family can tell you aren't on one accord they will be leery about treating your spouse equally. You're showing them you aren't on the same page. In their minds you may not even last and they shouldn't even put forth much effort to include your spouse in any of the family's ventures.

Heated arguments and heavy disagreements should only take place in your house. When they occur in front of family members your family members get to see the fight but they don't get to see you make amends. The next time they see you together they will assume you are still fighting. That's the picture you left on their minds.

Most families have a family portrait on the wall somewhere in the house. Usually, it's the big picture in the family living room. Every time your spouse visits your family your spouse is reminded how they are excluded from the pictures of your past. All your spouse really wants is to stand next to your siblings and feel completely equal the next time a full family picture is taken. Your spouse will never fit into your family's past but your spouse has every right to be included in your family's future.

7
Selfies

Most cell-phones have a reversed camera. It's the camera setting which allows you to take a picture of yourself. "Selfies" are the new fetish sweeping the world.

I remember when people had pictures of their kids in their wallets, between the pages of their bible, and even on the dashboard of the car. Well, today, things are different. Slide over kids. "I wanna look at myself all day!"

When you go out to eat and someone in your party asks, "Excuse Me. Where's the restroom?" 9 times out of 10 they don't really have to use the bathroom. They are going in the bathroom to take pictures of themself to post on a social network site. It took a lot of work to get that hair fixed up like that. That person spent hours putting the right outfit ensemble together. They are going to die if they don't show their followers their "ducklips" in the mirror of an elegant Ruth's Chris bathroom.

Green Means Go

People even do it while they drive. I have literally seen people post selfies on Facebook and Instagram (which would be normal in most instances) but it's ridiculous to take selfies while you're driving. They do it all the time. People are blowing behind you at a stoplight because you're sitting there trying to get the right pose for your selfie but the light has turned green. Now, you're holding everyone up at the light just so you can see yourself looking sexy with your hands on the steering wheel.

It's an obsession and at times it is an addiction.

Reflection

I love advanced technology. It's very helpful to have a camera setting which allows the camera to show you your own reflection. Many times it really   is a good mirror. In fact, that's one of the reasons the setting was created. Mirrors on the face on the phone would give off glares that may affect you negatively if glares shine at the wrong time. Like driving. But having a self faced camera is not a bad idea to use for a mirror.

The growing fetish for Selfies is actually a picture of modern culture. Most people are in relationships but there is a secret agenda which they will never admit. Most people are only looking for someone to make them happy. Selfies are natural examples of what most people care about... themself.

People aren't concerned with being a positive role model anymore. Most people will do whatever it takes to retain a false sense of happiness... even if it means to degrade themselves and break every moral code they learned growing up. Nobody is ashamed to be selfish anymore. It's actually popular. Say whatever. Do Whatever. Be Whatever. Offend Whomever. Cover it all up with the idea life is short and we must do whatever it takes to be "happy".

Look At The Picture Closely

All that sounds cute for a scripted Reality TV Show or maybe on a cool T-shirt you'd buy on a corner in New Orleans or New York but in real life you don't get to do whatever you want to do to be happy. When you're single, you're heavily influenced to live it up and be happy. It's so addictive that you assume you're supposed to have that same happiness when you find that special person. When you find that special person you'll immediately realize it's not just about you anymore.

If you want a real Selfie, look at yourself for real. Then, ask yourself. Would you want to be in a relationship with you? Just maybe what your lover is saying about you is true. Maybe you do nag more than normal. Maybe you do frown a lot. Maybe you are insecure. Many times we neglect to see the truth about ourselves because when we look at ourselves we are specifically looking for only our best attributes. Truth is, those ugly attributes are staring back at you simultaneously with all the things you love about yourself. Because we get so comfortable with self we train our minds to tune out the parts of self which could use tweaking.

Look at your *self picture* closely. Attempt to see what other people see when they look at you. Overlook your pretty skin and your radiant smile. Look at the way you frown when you raise your voice. Look at how bossy you come across to others when you demand things go your way. Look at your lack of compassion for what others may be going through at times when you are all about yourself.

College

When you are planning a future with someone you shouldn't just ask yourself if you can spend the rest of your life with that person. You must also be honest and ask yourself can they spend the rest of their life with you? When you're together you have to deal with each other. Strengths and weaknesses. There is no need in someone else trying to live with a personality that you can't even live with yourself.

When I was in college, I had roommates. We were the best of friends at times. Other days the smallest thing caused the biggest disputes. There were days we almost had fist fights over something very childish. My friend, Mike, and I always stirred up

42

heated arguments. We'd go days without speaking to each other. It took about two days for things to settle and we'd act like we never 'cussed' each other out.

The difference is we were just roommates. He had his own room and I had my own room. We didn't have to see each other at night. There was no need to even talk. If he didn't want to talk to me he didn't have to. If I didn't want to talk to him I didn't have to. We were just buddies. Roommates. He had his own life. So did I.

However, when you're in a relationship with someone you can't act like roommates. You don't get the privilege to go to your room and not come out. You sleep in the same room and in the same bed. Going to bed mad is like leaving food out on the counter all night. You can ignore it if you want to but soon or later you will have to put it away.

Monitors

When two people are truly in love it becomes normal to monitor each other. "Baby, I like the way you wore your hair today." She doesn't have to look at herself as much if she knows you are observing her for her. "Honey, it looks like you're losing a few pounds." He won't need another woman to make him feel good about himself if she makes him feel good about himself all the time.

The only reason people are so hypnotized by selfies are because selfies make them feel beautiful. But, if someone else has a pattern of telling you you're beautiful then there is no need for you to poke your lips out in front of your own camera all day to take selfies. Communication is the key to a consistent relationship. If I'm making a daily effort to uplift you it means I have to pay attention to you. If you make a daily effort to uplift me you'd have to pay attention to me daily.

43

Usually, the people who are stuck on themselves get that way because nobody else is stuck on them. Somebody has to do it. Your spouse will either give you good attention or you will eventually accept good attention from the wrong person.

8
Airplanes

Nobody gets on an airplane expecting it to blow up. Most of us have just as much Faith as we do Fear. We just choose to embrace Fear. Sometimes, hiding behind Fear is much easier than muscling through Faith. Even though we don't expect the airplane to crash we still board it knowing there is a huge possibility it could.

Marriage can be very frightening. Love interrupts right when you're getting used to yourself. It's quite normal to second guess giving all of yourself to someone else. Even though we comfortably say we love each other there is always the idea in a far corner of the back of your mind... what if this plane crashes?

Love is not about giving up anything. It's about gaining something valuable. Commitment is the front porch of character. When others see your commitment to your spouse is authentic you instantly earn their respect.

Fear Of Flying

People who are fearful really want to be faithful. Most times they fail because they've never been exposed to true commitment before. Many marriages they have known ended very ugly and it only made them even more afraid to commit. So, when they see someone else in an obvious true commitment they give them respect.

They see a Partnership. Two people passionately working together is attractive. It's actually sexy. In fact, what makes a sex scene seductive is how two bodies work together to create a magical moment. Two lives working together to build a vision is very, very attractive. Don't be fooled. Almost everyone on the planet wants this. A man wants a woman who is capable of adding to his vision. A woman wants a man who will support her goals and she'll provide a role for him within her vision as well.

Fearful people also see Loyalty. The average person has shared their body and their heart with numerous people before marrying their Spouse. The idea that my body and my heart is under total jurisdiction to one person only is inconceivable to people who are afraid of commitment. But, they are consumed with desperation for the same act of loyalty for their own life.

They are also mesmerized by the Comfort of Acceptance. Single people are constantly trying to be perfect. Married people perfect each other. The dating scene constantly changes and it is a constant headache trying to keep up with the expectations of the next candidate. You change something about yourself for someone only to find out the next person doesn't even like it that way. It is nerve-wrecking.

When you're in a committed relationship, your spouse has grown to accept you the way you are. It takes a lot of weight off your back knowing sudden changes won't prompt permanent changes. Don't be afraid of change. Embrace it. Change matures us unexpectedly.

Terrorists Aboard

Airplanes are not 100% safe. There is always that possibility they could crash. Interesting though... if one of the pilots doesn't cause the plane to crash then usually it's because they allowed someone to board the plane who only wanted to see it crash.

That's why passengers don't belong in the cockpit. You don't know what their intentions are.

A terrorist is a person who looks normal but they have a secret agenda. They are boarding your plane to crash it.

Don't tell your girlfriends how good your game is if she hunts in the same woods you hunt in.

Married people will learn within the first 3-4 months you can't discuss the details of your marriage with your single friends. Most of your friends will not expect your marriage to last anyway. Women should never discuss sexual details about your husband with a friend. If you tell your girlfriend how good the movie is eventually she will want to see it for herself.

Husbands should never discuss the fragile areas of their marriage with his single friends. The single person won't view marital issues the same way. They have liberty to walk away and just not deal with a matter. You don't. The married man has to deal with every complex situation immediately because other lives are depending on his response to each struggle.

You will find yourself slowly drifting away from some of your friends. Their motives will begin to stand out. Smug negative remarks and lack of compassion for your new life will push you away. Don't even get upset about it. Expect it and be prepared when it happens. When terrorists take over an airplane we aren't alarmed because there are enemies on board. We are mostly upset because we didn't see it coming.

9
Mates

Not only can you live the life you plan to live with your spouse but you can live even better.

I'm sure many of the people you admire planned to be successful but I don't even think Jay-Z and Beyonce saw their current level of success coming. I don't think Brad Pitt and Angelina Jolie imagined they'd be over the top successful. President Obama surely planned for it but he and Michelle surely wake up overwhelmed each morning by the blessings which have been showered upon them.

There are many examples of people who are successful walking totally different paths but the couples who stand out to the world are the few who figure out a way to connect paths.

Let's take Jay-Z and Beyonce for example. She is worth a fortune by herself. So is he. Now, imagine how much those fortunes are worth together. Their children will never struggle and their parents have figured out a way to conquer the entertainment industry... together. They are very successful individually but life is much less complicated and much easier to navigate when someone compliments your journey.

Most people search for Soulmates. It sounds cute. "Oh I have found the person who connects with my soul." God is your Soulmate. Nobody on the Earth will ever know you better than The Creator does. I'm still trying to figure out what people are expecting to find. What you should be looking for is your Help Mate.

Marriage is a Religious Engagement. It's Holistic by design. Christ Jesus promises to return for His bride. The Holy Bible considers His Church the bride. Marriage is the example He placed on Earth to remind us of His relationship with His Church. The wife submits to her husband just as the Church submits to Christ.

Submission Is Not Slavery

Submission scares people. It has been taken completely out of proportion. Submission doesn't mean a woman becomes her husband's slave. It means she respects him as her leader and she is willing to follow him even if she doesn't understand his decision. No more than that. It doesn't mean she can't share her opinion. It doesn't mean she can't be the family's financial manager. It doesn't mean she can't vent aloud and express her feelings when she's upset. It doesn't mean she can't work if she wants to. It just simply means even if she makes more money than he does she still respects him as her leader.

Leadership doesn't mean the husband can make decisions without considering his wife's opinion. In fact, he should respect her so much that he refuses to make a decision without considering her perspective. It doesn't mean he is the best financial planner. It doesn't mean he is the best home improver. It doesn't mean he knows more about everything than his wife does. It simply means he will navigate the way for his family and she trusts him to get to the Promise Land even if the walls fall down.

Every religion protects the sacredness of marriage. While many religions have different traditions for the wedding ceremony the respect for marriage is shared across all Faiths. For Christians, marriage is one of the highest honors even though it is not even required. If you're still single you are just as important to God as someone who is married. The Apostle Paul writes in the Holy Bible, God would rather us all be single so He can have our undivided attention. (1 Corinthians 7:8-9)

Sex In The White House

President Barack Obama has probably crossed paths with many gorgeous women on his journey to the White House. Many of those women may have tempted him. Just because he is President doesn't mean he isn't still a man. Men can separate sexual needs from the needs of the heart. Sometimes, women have trouble dis-associating the two. Most women believe you have sex with the person you love ONLY. Most men view sex as recreation. When a man has sex with another woman and he says she is not important, honestly, she may not be. What she offers is the only thing he cares about. A man is never giving up his Help Mate for his Sex Mate.

If you are a man's Sex Mate just know you are important but unless you prove his Help Mate is inadequate you will never be Most Important in his life. A man's future is connected to his Help Mate. The only time he will choose his Sex Mate over his Help Mate is when his Sex Mate starts performing the responsibilities of a Help Mate better than his Help Mate.

President Clinton fell short of his marriage due to his sexual encounter with his Sex Mate. The man is not crazy. He wouldn't have achieved a fourth of what he achieved in power without his wife, Hillary. His wife was his Help Mate. Isn't it interesting even after the infidelity Mrs. Clinton took her private time to grieve but she never left her husband. Even though he cheated on her she was strong and mature enough to understand he was still her Help Mate. His infidelity didn't disqualify him from the role he pledged to play in her life.

50

Your Help Mate is not going to be perfect. That person is just the most qualified person on the Earth to perfect you. Many times your Help Mate may not be the most attractive person you know. That person may not offer you the best sexual experience out of all of your previous sex mates. That person may not even be as gentle with your feelings as some of your very good soul mates have been. However, your Life Purpose seems to be wrapped all around this specific person and you feel a divine connection between your future and the person you know is spiritually assigned to your life.

You don't settle down with someone because they are the sexiest. You don't buy a ring for someone because she can give you pretty babies. You don't say "Yes" when he proposes just because he is wealthy. You say "Yes" to the person who connects with your life purpose. Your Help Mate means exactly that. It's the mate who can best help you pursue your Life Purpose.

Scavenger Hunt

Natalie loved hanging out with her friends in the neighborhood. She grew up very close to them. Interesting enough though, her closest friends were all guys. One day she and her three guy friends participated in a Scavenger Hunt set up by the local recreation center. The winning team would get to intern at the recreation center for the rest of the Summer. This was a big opportunity for a group of early teenagers.

Natalie really wanted to win because she'd always wanted to be a lifeguard at the recreation center's swimming pool. She figured winning this scavenger hunt would give her an easy shot at learning how to become a lifeguard.

As the four teens followed the map they were given they began arguing amongst themselves half-way through the scavenger hunt. Tony controlled the compass. Henry decided

Tony was leading them the wrong way. He tried to convince the others to follow him. It was very hard for Natalie to ignore Henry because she secretly had a crush on him. Despite her hidden crush she decided to stay with Tony and stick to the course.

A few minutes later the other friend, Daniel, decided he knew a shortcut. He tried convincing her to follow him. It was hard for her to ignore Daniel as well. Daniel has always been one of her best friends. Usually, he is the first person she calls to hang out because he lives closer to her than the others. Despite how close she was to Daniel, she decided to stay the course with Tony.

Tony wasn't her crush and he wasn't as close to her as Daniel but he was smart. She knew he had something the others did not have. Tony had the map and the compass. She knew if she wanted to ultimately achieve her goal she would have to trust Tony to lead her because he had the missing link to what she really wanted. She really wanted to be a lifeguard.

When she and Tony won the Scavenger Hunt all the other friends were jealous. Daniel wanted her to come to the mall with him but she told him she'd have to catch up with him later. Her crush, Henry, asked her if she'd like to get ice cream. Normally, she would've melted inside just to hang with Henry but she told him, "maybe another day." Henry asked her what she had planned for the rest of the day and she responded, "Tony and I are taking a swimming class today so we can learn to be lifeguards." Daniel and Henry thought is was a waste of time so they walked off leaving Natalie standing there with Tony.

It didn't matter what her friends thought about her, she wanted to be a Lifeguard. She followed her right mind and stayed beside the only person who could help her get there. The more they worked together the more attracted she became to him.

The Puzzle

Most people spend so much of their Single Life looking for a good Sex Mate that they convince themselves the person who makes them feel good sexually is their Soul Mate. Because so many people don't have a close relationship with The Creator of their souls they look for people to fill the emptiness of their souls.

You simply have to know who you are before you agree to spend the rest of your life with someone. They have to know who they are as well. Both of you have to have an idea of how you can grow together. Then, you make a life decision to accommodate each other to the destination.

We were only created to operate in our Life Purpose. No man should even think about asking a woman to marry him if he doesn't 100% understand his own life purpose yet. It takes time. Some people receive the revelation of their life early. For others, it takes a few decades.

A woman should never marry a man who doesn't know his purpose. She can befriend him as God reveals it to him but she should stand her ground until he realizes it. Her only reason for marrying him is because she sees her place within his Life purpose. He should see his place in hers.

It's like a Puzzle. You get all the way down to the end and you're missing a piece to the puzzle. Your spouse should have that missing piece. If you can finish the puzzle without your spouse you don't need to be married. The only reason you need to marry someone is because that person is the piece you're missing.

What To Look For...

When you're dating you are looking for your Help Mate. You shouldn't be looking for a Sex Mate or a Soul Mate.

When you meet a person who knows their Life Purpose you will know instantly if you fit in it or not. If a man wants to go to the moon you may not be his Help Mate if Science is your least favorite subject. Every time he talks about becoming an astronaut you'll think its boring and you'll tune him out. It doesn't matter how attractive he is to you why force yourself into a role that clearly is not important to you?

Maybe a man has fantastic ideas and his ideas really intrigue you. When you're on dates he is always talking about visions and potential ideas he plans to launch one day. While dating you eventually realize he is a visionary with a brilliant, innovative mind but is terrible with paperwork and business administration. These happen to be your areas of expertise. You're very good at laying the groundwork for start up companies. The more you talk the more you realize you two can be great together.

Swim

When two people are connected for a greater purpose you begin helping each other as you grow with each other daily. The more you work with each other the more you care for each other. Now, your Help Mate has also become your Soul Mate. The more you care for each other the more you want to please each other completely. Then, your Help Mate who became your Soul Mate will also become your Sex Mate.

Everything you want will come full circle when your desire is to simply operate in your Life Purpose. If couples ever wander away from each other the purpose will always be the easiest way to bring you back together. Don't waste time swimming in your differences. Swim back to the Purpose. Your Life Purpose will always be your raft in troubled water.

10
Taste

Commitment plays in the same ballpark with Responsibility. They're on the same team. If you're going to be in a committed relationship don't jump into it by being irresponsible.

Beware of the friends who show you how many diamonds are in their wedding ring. It means absolutely nothing. Divorce is higher than the rate of Marriage in most states because most Marriages begin in debt.

An expensive ring doesn't guarantee the marriage will be successful. The wealthy and famous are divorcing every day. It doesn't matter how sexy a person is, immeasurable debt is not attractive.

The ring is just a symbol of the commitment you make to each other.

Fancy Rings & Big Dreams

When my wife and I married my ring cost me $39. I bought it at a ring kiosk in the middle of the mall the morning of the wedding. The number of diamonds in the ring just wasn't that important to me. I knew the following week all of our bills would be due. So, I had to choose between the ring and the light bill. I chose the lights.

Some people would say I was very cheap. I like to think I was frugal. The ring may look good but it wouldn't look so good to my wife if the lights were off a few days after the wedding. More importantly, as Head of my Household I would feel like a failure to have $5000 on my finger but can't even manage to pay an $80 electric bill. Financial Instability will bother every nerve within a *Real Man*.

People invest tons of money into wedding ceremonies but neglect to invest anything into their relationship. It is ridiculous to work an average job but get loans to have a showcase wedding which leave you drenched in debt afterwards. Who are you trying to impress?

Weddings have become the new Proms. From hair to makeup, gowns to jewelry, every woman wants a night to remember. But at what cost?

When The Fabulous Wedding Is Over...

Unless you are very well established financially, it takes most couples 2-3 years just to recoup the funds they poured into their wedding. What makes matters worse is the bride's family is responsible for the largest chunk of the wedding expenses. The bride's expensive taste not only prohibits her own marriage from launching properly but she also puts a heavy strain on her parents who will do anything to make her happy. Many parents take out loans to cover their daughter's wedding expenses. They are hurt the most when a couple gets divorced within six months to a year. They feel they wasted their money.

My wife and I tell people all the time, "if we could go back and do it over we wouldn't have even had a wedding". We were like most excited young couples. We rented the Convention Center and invited everybody we knew. We wanted the wedding to look like Paris. Every seat had to have a customized cover and the colors had to coordinate with the decor of the room. The food had more options than the local buffet. The hostesses and hosts were dressed like servers in the finest restaurant in town. We laid out a huge spread of gifts for our guests.

It was the talk of our social circle for months. Then, as the months passed it became less and less important. By the end of the year it was history and nobody cared about it. Somebody else was getting married and our wedding was yesterday's news. Luckily for us, my mother is a professional wedding coordinator. Much of our wedding expenses were consolidated because we didn't have much to buy. My mother kept a warehouse full of wedding decorations and we pulled from her inventory. Had we paid for our wedding it may have cost us $30-40,000.

If my wife and I could do it all over we would have a private exchange of vows with our preacher followed by a big family dinner at a local restaurant. Everyone in attendance would pay for their own food. Every man would be a best man and every woman would be a bridesmaid. Nobody would be left out and nobody would be broke. It would have been much less stressful and much more simple to accommodate everyone.

Those who have more can afford to do more. Take a look at your bank account and be serious with yourself. Can you afford to splurge?

What's more embarrassing, a small wedding or having to borrow money from your friends as soon as the wedding is over? If you live check to check there is nothing wrong with being a hardworking, responsible adult. You have nothing to feel ashamed of. However, shame will overtake you if your marriage fails due to your taste being higher than your means.

11
Practice

Shaquille O'Neal, Lebron James, and Dwight Howard are outstanding professional basketball players. They are actually "Freaks of Nature". They are giants compared to their peers. They were given a supernatural blessing at birth... Strength. These guys are monsters. They are huge.

You can stand two whole people in front of Shaq and you'd still see him behind them. That's abnormal. Nobody can buy height. It's a God-given advantage. Just because these guys were born with a special gift doesn't mean they don't have to practice daily to accommodate their gift.

Marriage takes practice. Everything within your marriage will require practice. You don't become good at anything over night, despite how skilled you think you are at it.

Fact is, with everything in life, we must improve daily.

Perhaps you are good in the romance area but are slightly irresponsible financially. Most people don't consider themselves financially irresponsible but most of us are.

Shopping With Your Eyes

If you make between $10-25,000 a year you should never have less than $1,000 in your bank account. If you earn $26-40,000 a year you should never have less than $2,500 in your account. If you make between $46-70,000 a year you should never have less than $4,000 in your bank account. If u earn between $71-100,000 a year you should never have less than $6,500 in your account. If your annual income is higher... you do the math.

Most people shop with their eyes rather than their mind. You see something in a retail window and you buy it. Without even thinking, it is very common to just buy it. Most people figure they have money in their account and there is no reason they shouldn't just purchase something they like.

Just because you have $3,000 in your account doesn't mean you have $3,000 in your account. It may not kill you to buy a pair of shoes for $65 until your car breaks down. Suddenly, every dollar counts. Marketers make billions of dollars every year off of the hypothesis that most people will shop with their eyes instead of their mind.

Who Controls The Money?

In a relationship one person has to take the responsibility to be the money manager. This person should know your future plans and has the ability to keep you financially equipped to accomplish those plans.

The man may be the Head Of the Household but it doesn't mean he has to manage the money. The wife may be better at money management and there is nothing wrong with her being responsible for the family's financial records. We all love to think women are irresponsible in shoe outlets but men can be just as irresponsible in technology and sporting good stores.

It takes daily practice. Pulling back on this to strengthen that. Eating less of this to save money for that. Spending less time doing this to dedicate more attention to that. It doesn't happen all at once. However, day by day and step by step you learn to do better with practice.

Talk About Your Money

Communication is also developed with practice. If you're single you don't need to check in with anyone. It is your world and you don't need to provide any correspondence to anyone. Once you open the door to your world and invite someone else in you instantly become a partner in every area of your life where you were once the CEO.

You have to check in with each other throughout the day. Your spouse has the right to know what your daily plans are. Your spouse has the right to know what you spend money on. Your spouse has the right to know who you are meeting with, talking to, lunching with, or even texting. Your spouse has the right to know all your passwords. Your spouse has the right to know what you are thinking about. Every move you make includes your spouse.

If a husband takes $400 from the joint bank account to go to the casino and loses it all, it directly affects his wife. It's her money as well. If the wife takes $150 out of the account to go buy a nice dress and the husband doesn't know about it, it directly affects him because that's partly his money.

Is it really so hard to ask your spouse if it would be okay to use some money for a dress? It's not that the wife needs permission but its a simple practice of Communication. You're practicing how to include each other.

The money for the dress is not even the issue. You are learning to correspond with each other on little things. When a catastrophe presents itself it will be just as easy to stay on one accord. You've been practicing it all along.

Your spouse doesn't trust you over night. Your spouse is trained to trust you. "Baby, did you take out the trash?" Don't say yes if you didn't do it. She will always remember the one time you said you did and didn't. It won't matter how many times you do it after this. In the back of her mind you are CAPABLE of lying.

It's better for the long run if you just say, "I forgot." It's not what she wants to hear but at least it's not a lie. Any woman would easily take a forgetful man over a lying one.

Training Day

In the movie, Training Day, Denzel Washington plays a corrupt cop who takes a rookie cop under his wings as his new partner. The rookie cop is just thrilled to be a partner and wear his badge. He believes in the Police System and trusts his partner instantly because he was taught in the academy to trust his partner.

As their first day passes, the rookie realizes his partner couldn't easily be trusted. In one day he learned his partner was a cheater, liar, conspiracist, murderer, con-artist, crook, drug dealer, and a gangster. When he first met him he had anticipation of learning from him and trusting him at all times like he was prepped to do as an officer on duty. He learned very quickly trust isn't something you can be programmed to just give away freely. It is earned over time.

In your marriage, you are coming into a relationship expecting the best. You've been programmed beforehand to trust your spouse and most times by the time you marry you do trust your spouse. However, trust can evaporate into thin air very quickly. When it does, it's hard to get it back.

Practice telling the truth daily. Make good on your promises daily. She's learning to trust you and you are learning to trust her.

12
Surprises

While most working men assume women want everything in their lives in order, they forget women still love surprises. Actually, everybody loves surprises. If you take the time to surprise someone it means they have your mind occupied. There is nothing more beautiful in a committed relationship than keeping each other on the top of your minds.

Confidence

Swagger is the level of confidence you have in yourself. Confidence is the ultimate sex appeal. Women love to see a man walk as if the pillars of the Earth are kissing his feet. Most women love a man who knows what he wants and won't allow anything to stop him from getting it. Indecisiveness is usually an enormous turn off. If a man can't make a decision for himself then most likely he can't make a decision on her behalf.

There is a difference in knowing what shirt to wear with a sports jacket and knowing how to set goals and accomplish them. Just because a man doesn't have a sense of style doesn't mean he's indecisive. Some of the most efficient men in the world don't wear Tom Ford cologne or watches from Cartier and many of the most confused men in the world smell like money, dressed in Versace.

A woman wants a man who needs her opinion but isn't worried about it. He has to enjoy being who he is. She should feel stronger about herself by being connected to him. The overflow of his confidence spills upon her. She must never be able to look into his eyes and understand everything. His mystery keeps her interested.

When a man knows his worth he walks as if the world knows it too. When a man knows his potential he speaks as if he already has what he's trying to get. When a man sees future in a woman he treats her as if he has already won her. This level of confidence can be perceived as arrogant if a man has no character. However, if he carries himself with a pinch of humility it's surprisingly seductive and mentally magnetic. He can be ugly as sin but confidence has a way of making a woman overlook his credentials to fall desperately in love with his potentials.

At some point life will weaken him. There will be days he will lose the very attribute which attracted her. The right rock can bring down any giant. When it happens his woman must instantly rebuild him and pour into his Spirit. If she doesn't, he will place her in the category with everything else he feels is against him.

Soon or later he will rise up. Champions always do. Don't assume because your man is in a temporary forest he won't eventually navigate his way through the trees. It's not that he fights which make him a Gladiator. He's a Gladiator because only death can make him quit.

O.P.P.

Most times people neglect the opportunity to surprise each other because they honestly don't know how to surprise each other. You can't wait until Valentine's Day to shower each other with special gifts. Spontaneous gifts are little fire logs. When the fire starts dying you have to put another log on the fire to keep it burning.

Be Original. Don't ever try to duplicate someone else's surprise. A woman can instantly tell if her man's surprise was his idea or someone else's idea. A man will immediately know if his woman's surprise is especially for him or if it's just something suggested in a Cosmopolitan article.

You know the person you love better than anyone else. Being original prompts you to think about that person's heart and their interests. So, when you surprise them they know it was creatively inspired just for them. There are a lot of duplicates of the Mona Lisa but the original painting will always have what the duplicates can't get... The Story.

History records Lisa del Giocondo married the wealthy Silk Merchant, Francesco del Giocondo. The painting was supposed to be a gift for them as they moved into their new home together but also to celebrate the birth of their second son. Although many people have replicated the painting, hardly anyone can replicate the reason it was painted. For Lisa del Giocondo it was a special gift that her husband wanted to give her.

Be Practical. If the person you love is shy then there is no reason for you to organize a flash mob in a public place just to say I Love You. Your surprise should be realistic. You don't blow your partner's mind with the event. You'll blow your partner's mind with how much thought you put into it no matter how big or small the gift is.

I hate company Christmas parties if we're required to pull names to exchange gifts. People always buy each other generic gifts because you really don't know each other well enough to buy a personal gift they'd honestly appreciate. I have enough coffee mugs and ties.

I love the episode of The Cosby's when the husbands challenged each other to purchase gifts for their wives to see who was the most romantic husband. They couldn't spend more than $20 on the gift and the men would judge who is the most romantic by the level of surprise on their wives' faces upon receiving the gifts. Cliff Huxtable was the only husband who didn't try to buy a $20 gift. Instead, he found a barrette that his wife had wanted since she was a kid. The barrette may have cost him $1 but it meant the world to his wife.

Materialism will never keep you married. The ability to understand your spouse is a much stronger glue.

Be Personable. Ask yourself, what does your spouse truly enjoy? Center your ideas around the little things which make your spouse smile. If she likes a certain flower which doesn't grow in your region, getting it to her may hurt your pockets. However, you can send her a text attached with a picture of the flower and a personable special message. *Saw this and I thought about you. I just want you to know you're on my mind baby.*

Sweetness doesn't have a price. It's manufactured in the heart.

Women assume men only want Sports or Technology related gifts but we appreciate thoughtful gifts too. If you give your man a candle and a bottle of wine with a note that reads, *I'd like to light this candle and sip this wine with you in a nice bubble bath while listening to some jazz when I get home from work...* I promise he'd appreciate this small suggestive gift much more than a tie.

A woman tends to love surprises which suggest she is important to her man. Men always love surprises which promise intimacy somewhere in the near future.

Truthfully, it doesn't matter if the surprise is grand or small. The surprise is not the turn on. The thought does the job. The fact that you actually went out of your way attempting to make your partner happy is very attractive. Surprises keep your relationship interesting. As long as you are both secretly trying to surprise each other no one outside your relationship has room to distract you.

13
Empire

The way God designed the family has been bootlegged and repackaged by counterfeit distributors. The home should never have a single parent. People shouldn't have to go on Maury to find out who their baby's father is. There shouldn't have to be a child support system.

My worst nightmare is the idea of my sons waking up in another man's house, looking up to another man as "Daddy". That image in my mind frightens me. The fact that so many men are comfortable with it says a lot about the era in which we live. Everything abnormal is normal but everything God created to be the norm is now absurd.

The family is the key to improving the world. One reason we continue to build jails is because as long as we aren't building families we'll always need more jail cells. There is a reason why God designed the family the way He did.

Don't Pee On The Seat

My dad told me and my brothers if we continued to pee on the seat he would get some scissors and cut our penises off. It's funny now but as kids it was frightening. As harsh as that may sound we never peed on the toilet seat again. Even as an adult it is one of my pet peeves.

"When your mama has to use the bathroom can you imagine how discussing it must be for her to see urine all over the seat?"

It made us very considerate of the woman who lived in our home. So, when we had to use the bathroom we either lifted the seat or took the responsibility to wipe the seat before we left the bathroom. Although urine on the toilet seat is very grotesque, the lesson wasn't only about the nastiness of leaving urine on the toilet seat. My dad was teaching us how to live with a woman - even as young boys.

So many grown men today missed very important lessons like this one. This lesson wasn't just about peeing on the seat. It was also the beginning stage of learning to be considerate of others. Etiquette is something you can teach. Character is something you have to develop.

Close Your Legs Little Girl

My aunts taught their daughters to sit with their legs closed. I'm under the impression my grandmother must've used strict repercussions for my mother and aunts when they were little girls if they sat with their legs gapped. I've seen my cousins get tapped with rulers many times for sitting with their legs open especially in the company of boys.

"If you can feel the wind blowing between your legs then they are open too wide," I can hear my grandmother preach.

It was a reminder to them that they were young ladies. So, when they sat around us they would either cross their legs or at least pull their flowered dresses down over their knees with their legs pulled tightly together. Even though it wasn't very presentable for a young growing girl to show her body to mannish young boys, the root of the lesson my grandmother was teaching them is Self-Respect.

So many grown women obviously missed these important lessons because even as adults, many can't keep their legs closed. When a man meets a woman the first thing he should recognize is the respect she has for herself. If he instantly sees she has no respect for herself he's not going to pretend to care about her. Clearly, he doesn't have to.

Having Fun Or Settling Down?

When you're single and dating you know what you're looking for when you're out on the prowl. There is nothing wrong with dating for fun. Just Close Your Legs!

Dating should be fun. Meet new people. Develop great networking relationships. Companions in your field of interest can turn into future business opportunities. However, you don't have to sleep with every cute person you meet. You don't have to be promiscuous to date.

Most men who are somebody's "Baby Daddy" allowed a date to go too far. If you didn't have any condoms and you did it anyway it shows a lack of consideration for your own future. It doesn't matter if it is consensual or not. The minute you unzip your pants you choose that moment over the entire rest of your life. So, if you choose to unzip be very sure that the person you lay with is part of your future plans. Ultimately, the only reason a man and a woman has kids together is to expand their empire.

Finding The One

At some point we all decide we've been in the dating pool too long. We start dating with expectations of meeting a possible life partner. It doesn't matter how ready you think you are. Settling down can not be scheduled. It happens when it happens.

The key is to date with an open mind. Don't date with open legs. When you decide to hold out, the weak candidates will bail out.

You're supposed to spend a lot of time dating potential life partners. Every conversation matters. Every perspective matters. Every argument matters. These are all factors which determine what kind of family you can build with that person. You should be comparing life goals, worldviews, spiritual perspectives, parenting opinions, future plans, and anything that will give you an idea of what your life with this person would feel like.

Divorce continues to rise because people are having these conversations after they are married rather than before. After a child is born and you've bought a house together you get a sudden epiphany. *This is not the person I thought I married.* Truth is, it most certainly is the person you married. You just didn't know the person you married because you never asked the right questions when you were dating. Knowing his favorite color can't support you when his work ethic has to show up. Knowing her favorite song won't do a thing for you when you realize her political perspectives are the complete opposite of yours.

Having a child with someone is no reason to marry them. Unfortunate circumstances should never prompt you to marry someone. Marriage is completely about Life Purpose. Marriage should have already been in position before you had sex. The reason God prefers Marriage before sex is because when you marry someone you have supposedly already found your purpose and matched it with a Help Mate who identifies with that purpose. Together, you raise a child to be an offspring of what you both are building together.

People are confused about the order of the family today because they grew up in environments which presented them a different picture of family from what God designed.

It's hard to tell someone they can't marry someone of the same sex if they grew up in an environment where they hardly ever saw two people of the same sex stay together. In their mind, love can't possibly be what they were exposed to growing up.

It's hard for a young man to even consume the idea of having to be faithful to his wife and be active in his child's life when growing up his own father got away with simply paying Child Support. In today's generation, paying Child Support is an easy way out the responsibility. Send your money and you never have to even deal with it. Sadly, many men today find this option much more comfortable than actually having to be involved in a child's life.

Many young ladies aren't interested in submitting to a man and letting him lead her. She watched her mother do it all by herself and in her eyes her mother did alright. As an adult, she takes care of herself, makes good money, and hasn't had much need for a man to lead her. As a matter of fact, most of the men around her are intimidated by her success. She convinces herself she doesn't need a man and has become pridefully independent. Unfortunately, a man picks up on that energy very quickly. Most women don't even realize when they are waving their "Proud To Be By Myself" flag.

Our world has figured out how a man can change himself into a woman. We have figured out how to implant wombs. We have figured out how to add silicon to specific body parts to make them as big as we prefer. Science has convinced us that we can recreate the original design for many things around us. Because we have successfully created so much, it's no surprise we have adjusted the original family module.

Repairing The Breach

We must admit we're wrong. We see it wrong and we are absolutely out of order. If we can't even admit it we can't fix it.

Men must resume their responsibility as fathers. We must teach our sons the important lessons which will shape their character and consideration for others. Mothers must instill self-respect in their daughters at early ages. One of the tragedies of Dating today is not looking for someone who knows their Life Purpose. It's hard to even find someone with enough life essentials to parallel you in a moderate conversation. So many life lessons were never learned. Therefore, so many adults are still childishly dating at the age they should be looking to settle down.

The structure of the family is designed with each adult playing an equally important role. We have allowed the influences of the misguided to leave a tainted impression of the true family on our minds. It seems too hard to master so we accept alternatives rather than the challenge. We build jails instead of building Character. We build Abortion Clinics instead of Self-Respect.

The world simply band-aids the problem but restoring the family would repair the breach altogether.

I've said it many times. My worst nightmare is my son being raised by another man and looking up to him as "Daddy". We haven't even begun to improve until this same nightmare scares every man enough to make sure it never becomes his reality.

14
Mirrors

There is a reason we have two mirrors in one on the side view mirror. We need both images. One mirror is what we see up close. The other mirror is what we need to see from afar. We need both images at the same time.

The Closer Image shows you what is close to you. It's usually the biggest image in the mirror. The Distant Image gives you a glimpse of things which are not close but you still need to see them. In life, you need two sets of motivators. You need somebody close to you who will work with you from where you are. But simultaneously, you need someone from a distance to keep you focused so you can see how far you can grow.

One person keeps you on the road. The other person makes sure you can see the road ahead of you.

Life Work

Many people fail because they have the Distant Person but they don't have the Closer Person. The Closer Person is important. You can't go the distance if you can't even stay in the race. The Closer person helps you stay in the race.

It's good to have a celebrity couple or someone who is a community leader to follow. You identify with their Life Work. You recognize their purpose and it attracts you to their work from a distance. You'll never see these people fight or make love. You aren't supposed to. Their general purpose for being in your life is to show you and your spouse how to operate in your Purpose. You're supposed to mirror their work ethics from a distance.

In Marriage, Purpose is the bottom line and the top line. It's the beginning, the middle, and the end. When two people connect by purpose they will make it work on purpose. The Distant Examples keep you focused on your purpose. You don't need to be a spectator for their struggles. Pay attention to their mission.

Others fail because they have someone Close but they don't really have that Distant Couple to observe. While a closer couple keeps you in the race, the race could go on forever because there is no one giving you a clear image of the finish line. Somebody has to be the one who prepares you for the level of success you expect. They don't prepare you by being close to you. You're prepared by simply watching them from a distance.

Tell Me The Truth

The Distant Examples are important but so are the Closer Examples. You can't speak to the Distant Couple to receive purposeful life answers. The Distant Couple can't pray with you. The Distant Couple can't listen to you vent when your temper rises. The Distant Couple can't give you sound advice. The couple who mentors you has an important role. They have completely different responsibilities from your Distant Examples.

Every adult with a living parent should call your parent one day. Ask your parent(s) to tell you the truth. I called my father one day because he is more helpful to me alive than he will be in Spirit if I'm lucky enough to outlive him. Your parents' testimony is the explanation for many of your misunderstood life corners.

Ask your parent to tell you the areas in which they could've done a better job while raising you. You'd be surprised how much your life mirrors their life. We either learn to think just like our parents or we despise them so much that we purposely try to think completely opposite of them. Many of our life struggles are hereditary. Most of our parenting perspectives are trans-generational. Many of our marital ideals are subordinately influenced.

If you don't have parents alive or if your parents aren't eligible it may be wise to adopt a seasoned couple as your mentors. Search your church. Observe your neighborhood. Maybe an uncle or aunt somewhere in your family has a successful relationship. If so, begin shadowing them and ask them to mentor you and your spouse. We all need someone who can guide us through rivers they have already crossed and tests they have already completed. They help you where you are while the Distant Example shows you where you're headed.

Parental Guidance

It must be your intention as a Married Couple to lay down the path for your offspring. Family is less valuable today than it was 50 years ago. Half A Century ago marriage was honorable. It exemplified Commitment, Integrity, and Leadership. A married man had credibility in the workplace because the idea of Marriage alone carried so much Honor. If we restore Marriage we'd also be rejuvenating the family. Focused families produce better communities. Enriched communities produce enriched youth.

Many kids only go as far as their parents. Very few go beyond them. It should be every parent's purpose to make sure your kids grow with the essentials and opportunities to go beyond your own achievements. If they will grow up to live just like you then they should never even move out of your house. They'd do better to just help you do what you do.

Kids have to be exposed to people in the village who will mold and shape them for the world but they have to be consistently reminded that the village is not the world. Do not force a child to think like the village. One day, when he learns there is a big world beyond the village he will either be attracted to it so much he evolves or he will be intimidated by it. If the world intimidates him he'll find it easier to stay in the village and live no different than you. Comfort is often our worst curse.

You live in a village because you want to. You can't expect your child to enjoy the village just because you do. The more you glorify what you like the more eager they'll want to experience what you don't like. Personal experience shapes most of our likes and dislikes. Just because milk doesn't sit well on your stomach doesn't mean the whole world is lactose intolerant.

Missing Good Examples

The youth in this generation don't see many strong marriages in the village anymore. As a matter of fact, Co-Parenting is more common than Marriage. It's not uncommon for multiple siblings to all have different fathers. However, if you talk about the affect it has on the community at large society will consider you offensive and insensitive. We make excuses for ourselves but the decline of the traditional family has become the ecstasy of irresponsibility.

If you missed good examples within your home then your failure to keep a productive relationship is not entirely your fault. Your perception of the world may be small and your idea of true love may also be boxed. However, you can learn from it. Journey back through the experiences you've encountered. The experiences which profited you pain and sorrow were examples of how not to live your life. The experiences which brought you light may have been blueprints to help you build. The Closer Examples in your life are responsible for providing hands on experiences to build you whether good or bad.

Know that the Distant Image won't look exactly like the Closer Image. One is going to look clear because it is close. The other will be positioned just so you can see it enough to know its there. The Closer Image will sometimes wreck your nerves. You'll see it up close and you can tell what's wrong and right about it. Its spots will be easily noticeable. The Further Image has the advantage of being near perfect. You aren't exposed to its scratches. You see it in completion. It works out fine for you though. The less you know about the Distant Image the more you stay focused. The more you know about the Closer Image the more you stay grounded.

15

Tantrums

It is the nature of anything living to be an individual. We don't think the same on everything. Within every species there may be appearance similarities but eventually something will stand out.

Trees aren't the same height. Sand color is different depending on the climate. Rock structures are all different in size and height. Some mountains are more steep than others. Humans... well some of us can become *aliens* at any moment. One day you completely understand each other. The next day you have no idea who you're living with.

Two Of Everything

When our oldest son, Cadence, turned five years old we wanted him to have a big party. My wife and I agreed. Five was a milestone year and we wanted him to remember it. My oldest son is actually born on my father's birthday. So, we had a big party for them both at the beach. Our church and family friends brought gifts and food to celebrate with us.

Our sons are pretty close in age. They aren't even a full two years apart. Hey, don't judge us. We were in a groove and we popped them out back to back. If this were a social site I'd throw an "LOL" in right there.

Because our sons are so close in age they've always played together. We often tell people how proud we are of them. They play so well together. Sometimes, we have to check on them because there isn't any noise. We'll find them quietly playing with Building Blocks or Legos.

We learned a very important lesson about our sons that year. Until this Beach Birthday Party, neither one of our sons had ever been singled out. All of their toys were the kind of toys with multiple pieces. There were a box full of Building Blocks. There were tons of little race cars. There were gobs of little wrestling and ninja figurines. Most of the toys we bought had matches. If one kid had one the other one had one too.

When people brought gifts to the Beach Party they only bought gifts for Cadence. They didn't know any better. They figured it was his birthday so quite naturally he was the only person they needed to buy a gift for. Our baby boy, Ethan, threw the biggest tantrum we had ever seen because he didn't get any gifts. He didn't care that it wasn't his birthday. He was accustomed to being equal with his brother in everything.

Fact is, they were equal. Each brother had 100% access to each other's toys. They lived together. They played together. They ate at the same table. They slept in the same room. They felt equal until it was established that one had authority over something and the other one didn't. Ethan was not interested in hearing this arrangement and it became the root of every disagreement and fight from that day forward.

Acceptance

In a relationship, one person will be leader and the other person must completely accept submitting. In a Christian Marriage the husband is expected to lead the household. The wife is expected to submit to her husband. Within Christianity, it has more to do with symbolization than it does with gender inequality. The Christian Marriage is designed to mirror Christ and His Church. Christ is the Groom and The Church is mentioned as His Bride.

Homosexual partnerships are surprisingly respected by many Christians. Every person has the freedom to live with who they choose to live with. People reserve the right to love whomever they choose to love. A person has the right to share benefits with whomever they love, despite their gender. The area which causes the most conflict is granting legal homosexual partners the right to use the term "Marriage" to define their relationship. Marriage is Religious by definition. The actual definition of Marriage derives from the perception presented in Religious Theology.

Most Christians feel allowing Homosexuals to marry distorts the reason Marriage was ordained by God. Allowing two men to marry implies Christ saw His Church as His equal. Allowing two women to marry implies Christ was a woman. Either option subtracts truth from the Holy Bible. Paul records in the bible: God is the Head of Christ. Christ is the Head of Man. Man is the Head of his Wife. (1 Corinthians 11:3) The Husband in the Christian Marriage is depicted to be protector and coverer of the Wife in the Relationship. The bible clearly establishes one leads the other.

Most Christians clearly understand a person's right to live as happily as they please but many feel using the term "Marriage" out of context is a disrespect to one of the oldest customs of Christianity. Most Christians would probably support "Same Sex Legal Partnership". However, there are many Gays who are Christian. They believe due to their self identities the same concept of Christian Marriage applies to them.

Many Homosexuals have adopted the Christian concept. One person leads while the other accepts they must submit. In my opinion, it doesn't matter if it's a Traditional Relationship or a Contemporary Relationship. One thing is for sure. One person will be determined the leader and the other has to be willing to submit. It must be understood early in the relationship. If not, soon or later you will get to the point where somebody realizes the other has more authority over the toys. The lesser person will most definitely throw a tantrum.

World War III

The roles have to be established and accepted in the beginning of the relationship. They must be respected until one person proves he/she can't handle the responsibility. If you're the leader in your relationship and you fall short in an area it's obvious you need help. If you pretend you can handle it and the other person can clearly see you are leading them in an unhealthy direction you will launch World War III.

Just because you are the stove doesn't mean you will tell the fire how to burn. You may tell the fire when to burn but the fire is pretty capable of burning on it's own. A man's wife is not dumb because she submits. As a matter of fact, most times she has to be smarter. She has to watch the areas her husband looks over. She has to watch his blind-spots. Usually, his eyes will always be straight ahead. He won't even see most of the knives thrown at his back from his enemies. She will.

Dumb and Dumber

Don't ever make your wife feel dumb. If you do you better make sure you sleep with your eyes open. The minute you make a woman feel dumb or inadequate she takes on an instant obligation to make her husband feel what life will be like if she was not with him. Even though she submits to her husband, she shouldn't ever be ignored and disrespected.

If a man wants a woman to feel dumb actually he is dumber. The whole purpose of marrying someone is because they add value to your life. If you want someone to be dumb around you it doesn't say too much about you. If a woman plans to nag and talk down to her man it has absolutely no benefit to her. Why marry a man if you want him to have low self esteem? It's flat out stupid to pledge the rest of your life to someone you don't feel has enough sense to lead you.

If you want a pet get a dog.

"Dumb" people get married every day. They have no respect for each other. They lie to each other. Cheat on each other. Curse each other out. Steal from each other. Belittle each other with their selection of words. It's make you wonder why they were ever married in the first place. Maybe, it was cheaper than buying the dog they wanted.

Test Drive

The President of the United States may get ideas and hunches but he never makes a decision without consulting his cabinet. I honestly feel when you vote for a President you should know just as much about his wife's views. Most of the time she will have his ear before anyone else. Many of his past, present, and future decisions are decided with the person he trusts the most. Usually, it's his spouse.

A man will always keep a happy home if he makes his wife feel adequate even though she respects him as her leader. Consider her feelings at all times. You'll have to live with those hurt feelings. Consider her ideas at all times. If you don't, she will get a job somewhere and share all her aspirations to help build another man's company. Soon or later, she will talk to that man more than she talks to you. Obviously, he appreciates her mind more than you do.

It is important every woman considers the man she is dating very carefully before she commits to marrying him. Test him out in tough situations several times before you make a final decision to marry him. Observe how he thinks. Does he quit when facing a Red Sea or will he walk through it? If he never asks for your

82

opinion before you're married he probably won't do it while you're married. You need to decide before you walk down that aisle if you want to spend the rest of your life being a mute. Even dogs want to be heard.

People throw tantrums when what they are accustomed to is suddenly changed and they have no power to prohibit it from happening. In result, they can only cry about it. If you know what you're getting into from the beginning then you know what to expect along the way. A controlling person doesn't become controlling over night. Usually, there is a pattern. Take time to watch for it. It may not show up until you least expect it. If you're used to making decisions for your own household it's probably wise to settle with someone who makes similar decisions as you.

I wouldn't buy any used car before the salesman lets me drive it. It may have this and it may have that but none of it is important if it doesn't make me comfortable. I am the one who has to be happy with it once I sign for it. Obviously if it were perfect it wouldn't be on a Used Car Lot. Somebody has driven it and they have already found a reason to trade it in.

Other girls may have dealt with his attitude but can you deal with it? Other men may have dealt with her possessive behavior but will it irritate you? This is why you should date long enough to form a conclusion. If you marry someone knowing how they are, don't get all "brand new" after the wedding. You test drove the car before you bought it and you knew it was a used car. It will make absolutely no sense at all to throw a tantrum when the engine breaks down if the light was already on when you bought it.

Of course you're attracted to the things you love about someone but can you live with the things they do which get on your last nerve? Be honest with yourself. You can address your concerns before you're married or become an alcoholic trying to deal with it while you're married.

16
Breakfast

You can learn a lot by talking to your parents. If they could go back and change a few things they probably would. Most parents journeyed through life the best they could. There's that saying... *"If I Only Knew Then What I Know Now Things Would Be Much Different"*.

Imagine knowing what to expect in each season of your life. It sure would make more sense when the lamps start flying and moods start swinging. My dad told me life is a lot like breakfast. Know what to expect with each bite and you won't lose your appetite.

First 5 Years

The first five years of your marriage is like Rice Krispies. These first years will be full of adventure. It will feel like a roller-coaster. Some days will be so exciting you can't catch breath. Other days you won't have any idea what anything means. Other married couples will stand out to you. Your friend circle will change. You'll begin to fellowship with other couples as you recognize how much you have in common with them.

In the first five years, every sentence starts with "Bay" or "Baby". You will use those words for everything. "Bay can you get me some tampons while you're at the store?" Get you some tampons? Adding *baby* to the sentence doesn't make that sound any better! Bay this and Bay that. You will almost forget each other's real name. Other people will get sick of hearing you say it.

These years will be full of early romance and in the bedroom there's a whole lot of Snap, Crackle, and Pop. Young married couples can imitate porn stars. You are young and full of energy. Excitement permeates the bedroom. Everyday you can't wait to touch each other again. Buttons are snapping. Lips are crackling and bodies are popping. You are stuck on each other. Sex is the way you start the day and sex is the way you end the day. It's the way you'll approach your problems and after you argue, it is the way you'll solve your problems.

If you go to a young couple's house watch where you sit. They have baptized every room in their home with body sweat. Yep. That couch in the living room has been blessed by their holy body oils. The counter in the kitchen. They've cut up more than onions on it. It is a joyous time and you will spend the rest of your life trying to get back to this kind of Snap, the Crackle, and Pop.

These years will have a full share of arguments, fights, and disagreements. It is absolutely normal to want to quit twenty times during this season. Every time you have heated arguments you will wonder if you made a mistake by getting married. You will be tempted to tell friends hoping they can validate why getting married was a bad move. Each argument and each situation will only pull you closer. They will always present the perfect opportunity to have some more snap, crackle, and pop.

Second 5 Years

The second five years of your marriage will feel like Shredded Wheat. Where is the skip button when you need it?

These years are usually very tedious. Although these years will mature you they are hard to swallow. You'll both grow a lot in these years. Attitudes will change drastically up in here. Expect nonchalant mood swings all the time. Wives tend to be snappy about every little thing and husbands tend to forget everything that's important. It's not the end of the world. It's a natural reaction to relationship comfort. Guards are let down and the need to be perfect in front of each other all the time has slowly drifted past your address.

Usually, newlyweds have kids in their first five years of Marriage. So, during the second five years, the kids are going to school. It means mom is more than likely going back to work. Both parents have grown past the adventures of the first five years. Both parents have now refocused their attention on their careers. Time is not what it used to be. You'll rarely see each other. When you do, most times it will be in passing.

These will still be good years though. Your friendship will grow beyond measure. Your trust in each other will stretch. Your endurance will be tested and your support for each other will become even more substantial. Financial battles will force you to stay structured. Temptations will test your faith but you will learn just how much character you actually have.

These years come with sporadic pleasure and excitement. Intimacy will have to almost be penciled in on the calendar but it will still exist. You may have to squeeze in personal time while the kids are sleeping. You may even have to tiptoe around the house to find a quiet place at the right time. Because most of your time is now shredded into categories, intimacy is something you have to plan. The lock on your bedroom door will suddenly become the greatest invention ever!

10-20 Years

If you get to 10 you'll assume you can conquer anything. Just when you think the hard part is over, the stale part begins. Life will feel like Oatmeal. It will be warm and fulfilling but not exciting.

Your kids will grow up very fast in these years. Your marriage will also grow up quickly in these years. What he used to do to turn you on will now irritate you. What she used to do to spice up the bedroom will suddenly always happen at a bad time. You've gotten so used to each other by now that you don't even realize how often you sit on the stool in the bathroom with the door open having a conversation with each other.

Your looks will change. Although others noticed it long ago you will begin noticing it yourself. You really aren't as small as you used to be. Husbands aren't as strong and healthy as they were in their younger years. Many women gain weight and become slightly depressed at times. You always feel competitive. The young girl working at Burger King feels like a threat to you. *Even she is out to get your man.* You'll become self conscious about a lot of things. You may not even want to go to your Class Reunion.

You and your spouse will have survived a lot by now but you will often feel as if you missed something that everyone else had a chance to experience. You'll find yourself tired all the time. You'll be tired about everything. Tired of working. Tired of people. Tired of going to church. Tired of walking to the mailbox. Just tired for no reason.

Your spouse has long solidified himself as your best friend. You guys will laugh at things which no one else finds funny. At times you will lay in the bed too tired to even have sex but simply lying in the arms of the one you love is just as fulfilling. When you do have sex it will be better. By now you know exactly what to do and how to do it. You know exactly where to touch and how long to touch it. You just won't have as many opportunities to make love as you used to. Something always comes up or gets in the way. Most times it will simply be... you both are tired and worn out.

You'll be able to go on dates every now and then but they won't happen as often as you'd like them to occur. Dinner away from the house will almost feel like paradise.

Family issues will present themselves. You and your spouse will be called to help family members on both sides of the family. Health issues will present themselves and you'll have to wrestle through the hard times. Strangely you will feel happy and fulfilled just having someone by your side as you tread these waters. It will be a blessing to know you have security at all times but the season will be mushy. It'll be very lumpy yet gratifying but you will miss the snap, crackle, and pop.

20-30 Years Up The Road

A lot of people have started renewing their vows after two decades. It's not very common to last twenty years anymore. These years are the Fruit Loop years. For some reason it feels like Marriage starts over again.

For starters, your children will start leaving the house each year. You will finally get your house back. Just don't go changing rooms. They all seem to straggle back in from time to time though.

You can go back and make the loop to do some of the things you couldn't do while raising your kids. You will pick back up on hobbies and talents. You will be able to travel much more. You'll have a few extra dollars in your pocket at all times. It will almost feel unreal. Gas will stay in your car longer. Most of your bills will decrease tremendously.

You won't have as many responsibilities during these years as you have had in prior years. Sex becomes monstrous. It may not last as long as it used to but you will have it more often than you've been having it.

You'll start paying off many of your largest investments around this time which will free up a lot of your money. Usually, what your kids don't call and beg for is spoiled away on grandkids. Every time you hear from your kids it will bring back special memories. Seeing and hearing from your grandkids will brand smiles on your face even on your worst days.

There'll be some health scares during these years but you've gotten so much lost energy back you'll feel you can defeat anything. Your Faith is magnified during these years because you've survived many tests up to this point. Some days you will feel so young you'll actually forget how old you really are. The very things which made your life special when you first married seem to loop back around... even the snap, crackle, and pop.

Three Decades In

By the time you master sticking with somebody for thirty plus years there's nothing anyone can tell you about marriage. You could write your own book about it. You've endured a lot. Seen a lot. Gained a lot and lost a lot too. At this point life is a Continental Breakfast.

A Continental Breakfast is a fancy way of saying you won't get much of anything but you'll get a sample of everything. You'll get a little snap, crackle, and pop but you won't get it without some of the mushy oatmeal days. You'll get the benefits of your Fruit Loops but now the clock is ticking and you're shredding even more wheat.

Holding hands on the porch just may be the highlight of your day. Your kids' family has become the entertainment you need to get through the years. You'll live for the holidays. Being able to celebrate birthdays and anniversaries together become even more special to you. At times you may be able to loop around and enjoy some memorable experiences all over again.

You'll get joy out of sharing stories and lessons that will impact the younger people around you. You hope you have built a foundation in which your children can use as a model. Hopefully, what you've built can be passed to the next generation. It's an honor to see what Purpose has built. Ultimately, this is the only reason we get married in the first place.

17
Standing

My mother and I love going to Chinese Buffets. Even though we can't pronounce half of the food titles we still go. We'll try a little of this and we'll try a little of that. We're not bothered if some of it doesn't taste as well as we expected. We just don't get that particular item anymore when we go to the food buffet.

One day we went to a buffet we frequent whenever we're together and it seemed everything was just wrong. The buttered biscuits which are usually hot were hard and cold. The Low Mein tasted like it had been out on the buffet for a few hours. Everything was horrible. However, the next time I was in town we went right back to that same restaurant and things were like we first remembered them to be. As a matter of fact the food was so good we completely forgot about the one time it wasn't.

In your relationship you must be careful not to let one thing change your overview. One bad situation doesn't mean you have a bad relationship. I thought The Matrix Part 1 was great. I didn't care much for Part 2 though. Just because Part 2 let me down didn't change the way I felt about the initial concept. Your relationship is a concept. Every day you work hard to make the concept a reality.

Your Marriage is the way you want it to be.

Feelings

We care a lot about everyone else's feelings while neglecting our own feelings. Sometimes, you have to just call it what it is. If you are Co-Parenting and the engagement is stressful, you have to consider your own Peace. If you are a Step Parent and the other side is becoming a problem, you must consider your own Peace. If you and your In-Laws are at odds you must consider your own Peace. Letting issues continue to slide will only present a greater issue up the road. Don't hide your feelings until it's too late. Your Peace depends on your ability to stand and speak up for yourself.

Many times your relationship won't be destroyed by other people's actions. It'll be destroyed by your lack of action. There is a way to address a bothersome situation without being offensive. Even if the situation involves your spouse, you can address it in a moderate way. However, neglecting to address it at all only hurts you. Your spouse is going about life as if everything is fine with no idea you are even bothered about anything. Meanwhile, you are stressing over something that could be handled if you weren't so concerned with the feelings of everyone else without protecting your own.

Promises

There is an Acne Treatment Cream called Proactiv. There are many different solutions to prevent acne but what made Proactiv popular is its ability to prepare your skin before acne even showed up on your skin. Proactiv treated the skin with ingredients which fight off acne before it even settles into the skin.

When you stand at the altar and make promises you are being Proactive. You're making promises for the future. You are declaring to your spouse you will love them through Hell or High Water. You promise to stand with that person in sickness and distress, for rich or for poor, you are promising what your action will be in advance.

For some reason we are very proactive at the altar in front of the preacher but we become reactive as time passes. Being proactive will preserve your relationship. Address situations before they evolve. If you hear your brakes squeaking and the brake light comes on the dashboard of your car you should get the brakes repaired immediately. Don't wait for the brakes to go out while you're on the highway to finally take the problem seriously.

A great relationship is simply a series of meaningful acts.

From day to day you have to continue saying things to each other to build your fire. You must plan special dates throughout the year to give you both a focal point. Saying, "I Love You", will never go out of style. It's meaningful and it reminds your spouse that you haven't forgotten your promises.

Climbing Mountains

I've never gone Mountain Climbing but I've heard it is quite the experience of a lifetime. People have made a sport out of it. They strap those body braces around themselves and they will climb thousands of feet high. I watched an interview on the History Channel one day. A professional mountain climber explained the first time he climbed a mountain. He admitted he was extremely afraid. However, the more he climbed the less fear defeated him.

Relationships are full of mountains. Sure, you're frightened a little in the beginning. Perhaps the more you climb the more comfortable you'll be when you get tangled in the ropes. The more you climb the more prepared you become when rocks fall in your face. Maybe you won't be so nervous every time you slip. The only people who are afraid of mountains are the people who limit their life experience to the valley.

Life is better than you imagine it can be. It's more special than you give it credit. It's more fulfilling than you allow it to be. Just when you think you know it all Life teaches you something new. I'm kind of jealous of the mountains. They get to touch the sky without opposition from the valley.

When a couple exchanges rings it's a commitment to share a Purpose until death intercepts breath. We are born to operate in our Purpose until we crossover to the next realm of existence. Love just gives us a healthy companionship to pursue Purpose. Sex... well it's just one of the benefits included in the package.

In Canada, people visit the Whistler Blackcomb. They are two mountains which stand side by side. One mountain is called the Whistler. The other mountain is the Blackcomb. Skiers ski these mountains and tourists come to enjoy the mountainside each year. The Whistler is on the Southern Side of Whistler Village. Blackcomb is on the Northern side of the Village. When the mountains are covered in snow people rush to be near them. When the snow clears a different set of people come around to climb. People come and people go. The weather changes with the seasons and time may have changed their appearances, but one thing remains certain. Both mountains stand together.

60042170R00055

Made in the USA
Charleston, SC
22 August 2016